Contents

Is something lurking in this house?

A house is a place where you eat, sleep, work, and play. You sometimes read in your living room. But do you know what might be there with you?

In This Living Room

Nancy Harris

www.raintreepublishers.co.uk
Visit our website to find out
more information about
Raintree books.

To order:
☎ Phone 0845 6044371
🖷 Fax +44 (0) 1865 312263
✉ Email myorders@raintreepublishers.co.uk

Customers from outside the UK please telephone +44 1865 312262

Raintree is an imprint of Capstone Global Library Limited,
a company incorporated in England and Wales having its
registered office at 7 Pilgrim Street, London, EC4V 6LB
– Registered company number: 6695582

Text © Capstone Global Library Limited 2010
First published in hardback in 2010
First published in paperback in 2011
The moral rights of the proprietor have been asserted.

Edited by Rebecca Rissman, Nancy Dickmann,
and Sian Smith
Designed by Joanna Hinton-Malivoire
Original illustrations © Capstone Global Library Ltd., 2010
Illustrated by Kevin Rechin
Picture research by Tracy Cummins and
Heather Mauldin
Originated by Capstone Global Library Ltd
Printed and bound in China by Leo Paper
Products Ltd

ISBN 978 140621319 5 (hardback)
14 13 12 11 10
10 9 8 7 6 5 4 3 2 1

ISBN 978 140621325 6 (paperback)
14 13 12 11 10
10 9 8 7 6 5 4 3 2 1

British Library Cataloguing in Publication Data
Harris, Nancy.
 What's lurking in this house?. In this living room.
 1. Household pests--Juvenile literature. 2.
Microbial ecology--Juvenile literature. 3. Living rooms--
Juvenile literature.
I. Title
 579.1'7-dc22

Acknowledgements
The author and publisher are grateful to the following
for permission to reproduce copyright material: Alamy
pp.**11** (© Natural Visions), **7 moth, 10** (© Nigel Cattlin);
Ardea pp.**9, 13** (© Steve Hopkin); Bugwood.org pp.**14,
19, 29 beetle** (© Joseph Berger); © David Liebman p.**21**;
Minden Pictures p.**23** (© Stephen Dalton); naturepl.com
pp.**25** (© Colin Preston), **26** (© Dave Bevan); Photo Re-
searchers, Inc. p.**18** (© Pascal Goetgheluck); Photolibrary
pp.**17** (Oxford Scientific), **28** (Dennis Galante); Phototake
p.**27** (© Scott Camazine); Shutterstock pp.**6** (© Kati Mo-
lin), **7 beetle** (© Judy Crawford), **7 mouse** (© Thomas
Mounsey), **7 spider** (© theowl84), **29 mouse** (© Emilia
Stasiak), **29 spider** (© GeoM); Visuals Unlimited, Inc.
p.**15** (© Dr. Dennis Kunkel).
Cover photograph of a carpet beetle larva reproduced
with permission of Science Photo Library (Volker Steger).

Every effort has been made to contact copyright holders
of any material reproduced in this book. Any omissions
will be rectified in subsequent printings if notice is given
to the publisher.

All the Internet addresses (URLs) given in this book were
valid at the time of going to press. However, due to the
dynamic nature of the Internet, some addresses may
have changed, or sites may have changed or ceased to
exist since publication. While the author and publisher
regret any inconvenience this may cause readers, no
responsibility for any such changes can be accepted by
either the author or the publisher.

Some words are shown in bold, **like this**. You can find
out what they mean by looking in the glossary.

Getting cosy

You go into your living room and lie on your sofa. You open a book and start reading. It is nice to be alone with your favourite book. But are you really alone?

You might have more company than you think!

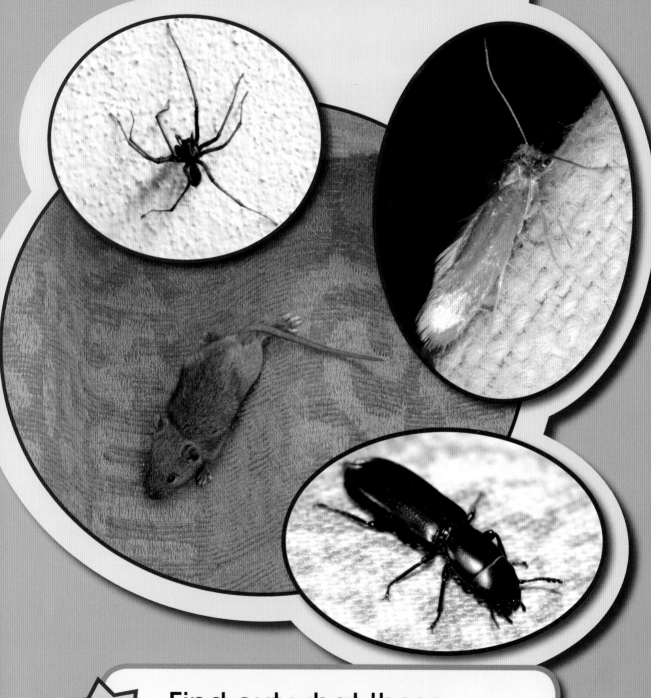

 Find out what these things are later on ...

Clothes moths

Young clothes moths are very hungry. They are called **larvae**. They love to eat wool and other cloth, or **fabrics**. They really enjoy dirty and sweaty cloth. Your fabric sofa is tasty to the larvae.

clothes moth larva

You can tell you have clothes moths in your living room if you spot holes in the sofa.

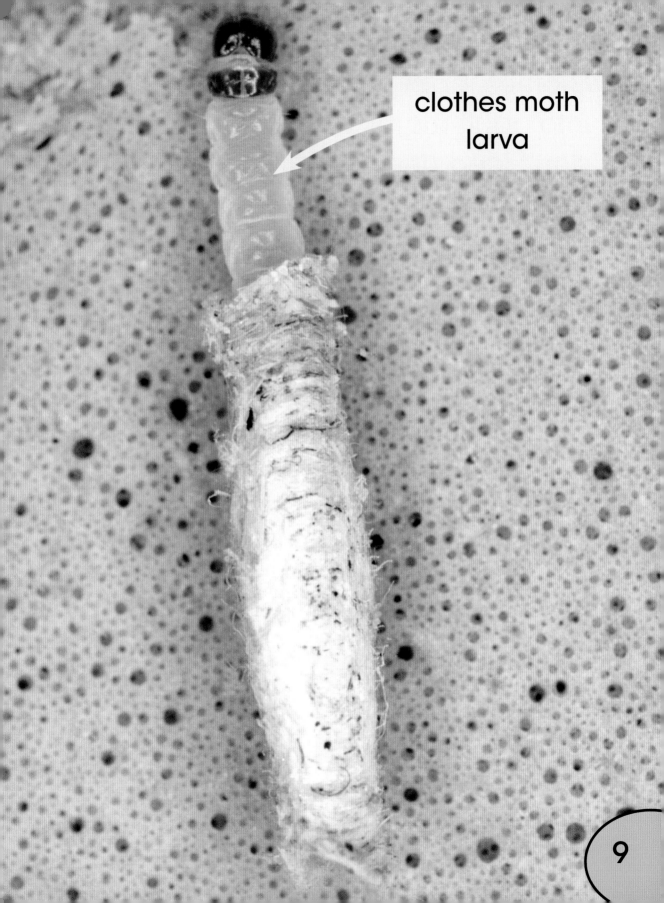

clothes moth larva

9

Clothes moth **larvae,** or young, turn into adult moths with wings. The adults don't feed on **fabric.** If you spot an adult moth, it is likely that larvae are busy eating somewhere nearby!

adult clothes moth

case

FUN FACT

Many clothes moth larvae build tubes called cases. They make these using silk threads, pieces of fabric, and sometimes bits of their own poo!

Hungry booklice

Booklice are tiny insects. They eat the glue that holds your books together. They also like to eat a type of living thing called mould. Mould can grow on the pages of books where it is **damp**.

booklouse

FUN FACT

Booklice are very small. Many are about the size of a pinhead.

Look inside the books in your house. Can you find a booklouse?

Beetles under your feet

Young carpet beetles called **larvae** also like to eat the glue that holds books together. Who would guess that it could be so delicious! They enjoy eating carpet and furniture **fabric**, too.

carpet beetle larva

This photo shows an adult carpet beetle up close.

FUN FACT

When carpet beetles grow, they **moult** or lose their old skins. They leave these skins lying around for us to find. Yuk!

Furniture beetles can also leave holes all over your living room. Young furniture beetles are called **woodworm**. They like to eat wood. They can live inside wooden furniture. They chew their way through it!

beetle

When a woodworm becomes an adult it makes a neat hole. Then it crawls out of the furniture.

adult furniture beetle

17

Eight-legged house guests

Look around your living room. Do you see cobwebs? House spiders make these webs to catch insects. Insects stuck in the webs make a tasty meal for the spiders.

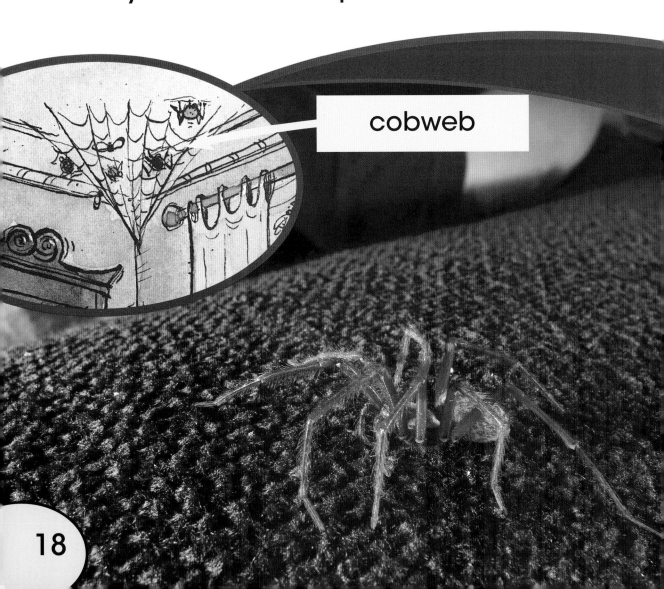

cobweb

Spiders can help to keep your house insect-free!

Eating webs

Plaster bagworms are insects. Their **larvae**, or young, live in cases they carry around. The larvae like to eat old spider webs. Sometimes they eat wool.

plaster bagworm cases

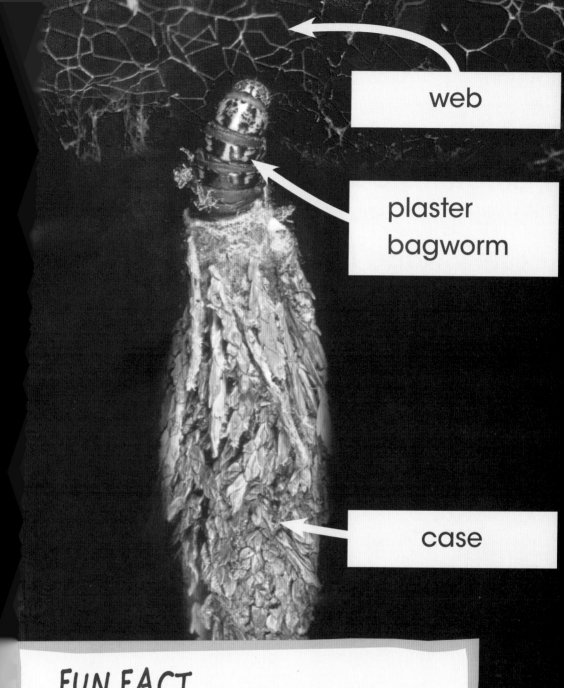

web

plaster bagworm

case

FUN FACT

Bagworm larvae make their cases from silk. They cover them with things they can find. This includes sand, dirt, or insect poo!

Squeak, squeak!

House mice are **mammals**. These furry creatures can get into your living room through holes and cracks. They might chew wood to get behind a wall. You know they are around because you can smell them.

mouse

FUN FACT

Mice will chew through anything softer than their teeth. This is bad news for wires in your living room!

wire

House mice usually come out and eat at night. They are **nocturnal**. If they come out in the daytime, they are easy to spot. Mice have tails that are as long as their bodies.

FUN FACT

Mice are great at climbing. They
have tiny hard plates on their tails
that can help them to grip.

Mouse meals

House mice eat many things they can get from humans. A few of the things they enjoy are:

- seeds
- candles
- cheese
- plants
- chocolate
- soap.

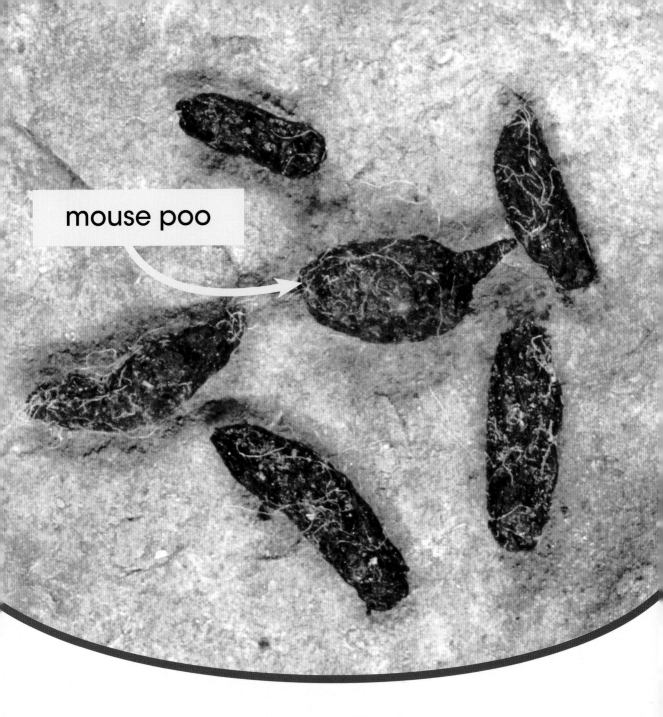

mouse poo

House mice even eat their own poo. There are things in the poo that can help them to live.

Keeping it clean

Make sure you keep your living room clean. Pick up food and crumbs. Vacuum the carpets and wash the curtains. This will help to keep the creatures out. Then you can sit in there and read your book without company!

Fun facts

House mice can walk along thin wires and ropes. They can also climb up rough walls.

Carpet beetle **larvae**, or young, are also called woolly bears.

A mouse's front teeth never stop growing.

When a male house spider dies, a female house spider will eat him.

Female clothes moths can lay 100 to 150 eggs. This means a lot of very hungry larvae eating **fabric** in your home!

Glossary

damp wet or moist

fabric cloth or material. A wool chair cover is a type of fabric.

larvae the young of some types of insect

mammal type of warm-blooded animal that gets milk from its mother when it is a baby. It also has fur or hair on its body.

moult to lose old, dead skin when new skin has grown underneath

nocturnal describes animals that sleep during the daytime and come out at night

woodworm young furniture beetles

Find out more

Books

All About... Bugs and Beetles,
Louisa Somerville and Maurice Pledger
(Silver Dolphin, 2007)

Germs, Ross Collins (Bloomsbury Publishing, 2005)

Usborne Beginners: Spiders, Rebecca Gilpin
(Usborne Publishing Ltd., 2007)

Where to Find Minibeasts: Minibeasts in the Home,
Sarah Ridley (Smart Apple Media, 2009)

Websites

http://www.pestworldforkids.org/beetles.html
Find out about carpet beetles and other types of
beetles on this website.

http://www.pestworldforkids.org/mice.html
This website tells you about mice in general and
describes two types of mice.

http://www.tooter4kids.com/Spiders/Spiders.htm
This website is packed with information
about spiders.

Find out

Which animals eat
15-20 times a day?

Index